The Literary Structural Analysis of John's Prologue (John 1:1–18 RSV)

as presented in

JESUS'S BELOVED DISCIPLE CALLING

SEIZE LIFE NOW!

LOU & NICOLE MERTES

The Impact Organization, Inc.
BELLEVUE, WASHINGTON

Published in 2017 by
The Impact Organization, Inc.
500 106th Ave NE, Suite 1801
Bellevue WA 98004

ISBN 978-0-9832421-4-7 (soft-cover)

Library of Congress Control Number: 2016954828

Cover & Interior Design by Scribe Freelance Book Design Company

PUBLISHER CATALOGING IN PUBLICATION INFO

———————

Mertes, Lou & Mertes, Nicole

The Literary Structural Analysis of John's Prologue (Jn 1:1–18 RSV)/ Lou Mertes & Nicole Mertes

1. Bible. N.T. John—Criticism, interpretation, etc. I Title. II. Volume

2. Christian life—Biblical teaching   I Title. II. Volume

BS2615   2017

Contents

*The essential thing is that the **verse structure should be represented to the eye**...where structural arrangement is wanting, no amount of explanation is likely to be of much avail.* [1]

—RICHARD G. MOULTON

[1] Richard G. Moulton, *The Literary Study of the Bible* (London: Heath & Co., 1898) 45

Part 1
John's Veiled Structures

TWO BREAKTHROUGHS

In the last century, scholars endeavored to bring more clarity to John's writings through research into his use of literary structures, but the results they hoped for didn't materialize. Some years later, we were introduced to the literary structures in John's writings, and we thought that avenue still had potential to produce more clarity. By building on the work of Dorsey,[2] Ellis,[3] and Breck[4], we made two major breakthroughs that we describe in this essay using the "Prologue" of John's Gospel as an example. We will demonstrate how we identified John's literary structures and how his first-century audience would have heard and used them as context for understanding his message.

HOW JOHN CUED HIS AURAL AUDIENCE

John alerted his auditory audience of interpretative clues by repetition and thought completion, which he accomplished by his placement of the following:

- Repetitive words and phrases
- Similar sounds
- Different words/phrases that have the same meaning

When John's listeners heard repetition or a distinct switch to a new topic, no matter where these items were in the scriptural text, they created a

---

[2] David A. Dorsey, *The Literary Structure of the Old Testament: A Commentary on Genesis–Malachi* (Grand Rapids MI: Baker Books, 1999)

[3] Peter Ellis, *The Genius of John* (The Liturgical Press, 1982)

[4] John Breck, *The Shape of Biblical Language: Chiasmus in the Scriptures and Beyond* (St. Vladimir's Seminary Press, 1994)

mental package of passages associated with these elements and used them as a context to understand his meaning.

The problem is that these interpretative cues don't leap out to people who read Scripture today. Scholar John Breck explains the reason—John placed these cues in a spiral movement rather than a linear progression.[5] With this said, let's look at the decoding process we developed to bring John's structures out from under the veil.

OUR APPROACH

Reverse engineering enabled us to identify John's own unique style of literary structuring. By making the intricacies of his structures visible through Microsoft Word tables, we could see how he wove layers of structures and substructures into integrated formations that revealed new interpretive insights. However, this method only took us halfway to our goal.

The ultimate value would be in the communication of the effects of John's structuring so everyone could understand his message with the same clarity as his first-century aural audience. This would require extracting and translating what was in tables into something readily readable. We liken this situation to what the scientists faced when they discovered the light bulb. They could get carbon to glow, but its light didn't last long enough to be practical, but Thomas Edison achieved that goal through his continued experimentation.[6]

Our continued experimentation in identifying John's literary structures also led to a practical solution. It was to "translate" John's work into what we call "RSAV" text (Revised Standard Aural Version),[7] to provide today's readers seamless access to John's words as he intended them to be understood. Those who are reading John's writings this way, note the positive difference brought by this newfound clarity.

---

[5] John Breck, *The Shape of Biblical Language: Chiasmus in the Scriptures and Beyond,*

[6] http://edison.rutgers.edu/newsletter9.html

[7] RSAV text is derived from the RSV translation; whereby, the RSAV converts the RSV into an aural formulation as first-century listeners heard and understood it.

HOW WE SHARE OUR FINDINGS

Our findings are based on two breakthroughs that led to our creation of a visible and replicable methodology. Our first breakthrough packages John's embedded and multilayered aural structures into integrated cells within Microsoft Word tables. The second breakthrough displays these aural structures as readable linear text. Our hope is that these templates will stimulate such excitement that they will become catalysts for further New Testament research.

We share our findings in two forms. This essay explains the methodology we used to discover John's structures. Our book *Jesus's Beloved Disciple Calling Seize Life Now!* displays the results of the structural analysis of what scholars deem to be some of John's most difficult-to-understand writings:

1. The "Prologue," the "Testimony of John the Baptist," and the "First Disciples" of John's Gospel
2. The "Farewell Address," which includes chapters 13–17 of John's Gospel
3. John's three epistles

Part 2

Identifying the Structures of the
First Part of the "Prologue"

INITIATING THE DECODING PROCESS

We begin by using word repetition and topic breaks to assess the structures that scholars who came before us identified in John's writings to discover the skeleton of John's typical three-part structural format. Each part supports interpretation by its own distinctive function.[8]

TABLE 1: THE FUNCTIONS WITHIN JOHN'S TYPICAL THREE-PART STRUCTURE

Label	Type of Passage	Function
A	First parallel passage	Introduces a thought or an idea
B	Point-of-prominence (POP)	Provides movement toward John's central meaning by presenting a turning point or a foundational point to convey where he is going and what to pay special attention to
A′	Parallel complement	Provides further explanation, elaboration, extension, intensification, comparison, contrast, fulfillment, or completion of the topic introduced in the first parallel

THE WAY THE THREE STRUCTURAL ELEMENTS WORK

We mark parallel passages in Microsoft Word tables by alphabetical characters to indicate their function. We start with **A** to designate the first parallel passage. We use the same letter primed **A′** to represent its complementary parallel passage. Identifying and displaying parallel pairs is

---

[8] John Breck, *The Shape of Biblical Language: Chiasmus in the Scriptures and Beyond, 33*

how John set up a topic and then explained what he wanted his audience to know about it, which was by way of a definition, description, or completion.

Typically, the two parallel elements act as two sides of a bun that surround the "meat," the key point, which receives the next alphabetical character as its label. Scholar Dorsey calls this passage a position-of-prominence[9] and rightly so, because John used it to reinforce his theme.

Displaying parallel words and ideas in tables by their function aids interpretation several ways:

- Repetitive words may be located some distance away from each other in scriptural text so displaying them visually helps a reader to see how they define the borders of a structure (see **table 2** below).

- Because these structural elements serve three distinctly different functions, seeing how they relate to each other as a first parallel, a parallel complement, and a point-of-prominence clarifies what John intended to communicate.

- Tables make it possible to detect and display substructures as cells nested within cells to indicate the correct progression in a person's consideration of the passages.

JOHN'S FIRST LAYER OF STRUCTURE IN THE "PROLOGUE"

The "Prologue's" overall structure, vv. 1–18 shown in the table below, is composed of two parallel elements and a point-of-prominence. We display this high-level structure because all substructures necessary for interpretation are derived from it. The repetitive words listed below define the boundaries of the "Prologue's" parallel elements **A** and **A'**. The topic shift between them vv. 11–13 defines the third element, the point of prominence of John's basic three-part structure.

- **"and the Word"** in vv. 1 and 14 (καὶ ὁ λόγος)

---

[9] David A. Dorsey, *The Literary Structure of the Old Testament: A Commentary on Genesis–Malachi* (Grand Rapids: Baker Books, 1999), 40

- "**made through him**" in vv. 3 and 10 (αὐτοῦ ἐγένετο)

The phrase "**and the Word**" opens the two parallel sections (**A** and **A′**). The phrase "**made through him**" establishes the lower boundary of section **A**. Word repetition clearly marks this segmentation, but does it make sense? Let's look at the topic each section deals with to verify.

Do the parallel sections relate to each other such that **A′** continues with the topic introduced in **A**? The answer is yes. Section **A** introduces the Word; the parallel complement (**A′**) tells us more, by stating what the Word came to do. A second way to verify this segmentation is to check for topic breaks. Verses 11–13 that formulate the point-of-prominence (**B**) clearly shift consideration of the Word to consideration of humanity by identifying what humans need to do and what they will receive.

TABLE 2: FIRST LAYER OF STRUCTURE OF THE "PROLOGUE"

John 1:1–18 (RSV)	
A (First parallel)	[1:1]In the beginning was the Word **and the Word** was with God, **and the Word** was God. [2]He was in the beginning with God; [3]all things were **made through him**, and without him was not anything made that was made . . . [9]The true light that enlightens every man was coming into the world. [10]He was in the world, and the world was **made through him**, yet the world knew him not.
B (Point-of-prominence)	[11]He came to his own home, and his own people received him not. [12]But to all who received him, who believed in his name, he gave power to become children of God; [13]who were born, not of blood, nor of the will of the flesh nor of the will of man, but of God.
A′ (Parallel complement)	[14]**And the Word** became flesh and dwelt among us, full of grace and truth; we have beheld his glory, glory as of the only Son from the Father . . . [18]No one has ever seen God; the only Son, who is in the bosom of the Father, he has made him known.

$\mathbb{P}$art 3

Identifying Substructures

THE PROCESS PROCEEDS IN A SPIRAL MOVEMENT

The initial cut of structure sets things up to probe for substructures. We start with the first parallel **A**. If there are no substructures, we skip **B** to probe **A′** the parallel complement for its substructures, before delving into **B**.

Label	Type of Passage
A	First parallel
B	Point-of-prominence
A′	Parallel complement

This is in accordance with John Breck's guideline that analysis should progress as first-century listeners heard these passages, which was in a linear **A B A′** sequence, but they mentally assembled them from the extremities going toward the center, in a spiral sequence.[10] When scholars comprehend structural elements this way, interpretation falls into place logically and elegantly.

IDENTIFICATION OF THE SECOND LAYER OF STRUCTURE IN SECTION A

Two repetitive phrases reveal the second layer of structure located in section **A**.

- **"in the beginning"** in vv. 1 and 2 (ἐν ἀρχῇ)
- **"with God"** in vv. 1 and 2 (πρὸς τὸν θεόν)

Even though these phrases are near each other, they indicate the existence of a substructure. The first parallel and the parallel complement passages of

---

[10] John Breck, *The Shape of Biblical Language: Chiasmus in the Scriptures and Beyond*, 29–37

the substructure shown in **table 3** below are labeled in a second column as **a** and **a'** to indicate this second layer of structure.

Notice the topic change in row **b**. The two parallel passages deal with the Word being "*with* God." The passage in **b,** the point-of-prominence, tells us something profoundly more about the Word, which is *the Word was God.* Modern readers typically treat these beautiful passages as only descriptions of the Word, but John used the point-of-prominence to support his main theme of the Gospel—the Word was God!

TABLE 3: SECOND LAYER OF STRUCTURE IN SECTION A

		Section A (1:1–10)
A	**a**	¹:¹ᵃ**In the beginning** was the Word, and the Word was **with** God,
	b	¹:¹ᵇand the Word was God.
	a'	²He was **in the beginning with God**; ³all things were made through him, and without him was not anything made that was made. ⁴In him was life, and the life was the light of men. ⁵The light shines in the darkness, and the darkness has not overcome it. ⁶There was a man sent from God, whose name was John. ⁷He came for testimony, to bear witness to the light, that all might believe through him. ⁸He was not the light, but came to bear witness to the light. ⁹The true light that enlightens every man was coming into the world. ¹⁰He was in the world, and the world was made through him, yet the world knew him not.

THE THIRD LAYER OF STRUCTURE IN SECTION A

There are no further substructures in **A–a** or **A–b**, but the repetition of two phrases located in **A–a'** reveal the existence of a third layer of structure indicated by the double-lowercase letters (**aa, bb, cc, bb', aa'**) in **table 4**.

- "**made through him**" in vv. 3 and 10 (δι' αὐτοῦ ἐγένετο,) reveals the parallel pair **aa** and **aa'**.
- "**light of everyone**" in vv. 4 and 9 (φῶς τῶν ἀνθρώπων·) reveals the parallel pair **bb** and **bb'**.

TABLE 4: THIRD LAYER OF STRUCTURE IN SECTION A: A–a′

			Section A–a′ (1:2–10)
A	a′	a	[1:1a]In the beginning was the Word, and the Word was with God,
		b	[1:1b]and the Word was God.
		aa	[2]He was in the beginning with God; [3]all things **were made through him**, and without him was not anything made that was made.
		bb	[1:4]In him was life, and the life was the **light of everyone**. [5]The light shines in the darkness, and the darkness has not overcome it.
		cc	[6]There was a man sent from God, whose name was John. [7a]He came for testimony, to bear witness to the light, [7b]that all might believe through him. [8]He was not the light, but came to bear witness to the light.
		bb′	[9]The true **light** that enlightens **everyone** was coming into the world.
		aa′	[10]He was in the world, and the world **was made through him**, yet the world knew him not.

These two sets of parallel pairs **aa** and **aa′** and **bb** and **bb′** sandwich the point-of-prominence **cc**. The first repetitive passage, "**made through him**," establishes the parallel pair **aa** and **aa′**; the second, "**light of everyone**," establishes the parallel pair **bb** and **bb′**. The first parallel **aa** describes the Word as the creator of all things. Notice that **aa′**, the complement, continues with the topic of the Creator Word that **aa** introduces to provide more information about it— the Creator Word was *not* known. This was John's set up for what he addressed next.

The topic shift in v. 4 indicates the existence of a second parallel pair **bb** and **bb′**. They introduce life and light as separate manifestations of the Word and state that the light is coming into the world. This is a logical progression of information from the **aa** parallel pair to the **bb** pair that indicate how the light will become known. Having completely considered the parallel pairs, we move to the point-of-prominence **A–a′–cc**.

THE FOURTH LAYER OF STRUCTURE IN SECTION A

Section **A** has a fourth layer of structure, which is shown in **table 5** below. It is indicated by the repetition of the phrase "**bear witness to the light**" vv. 7^a, 8 in (**A– a′–cc**), which creates a substructure with new alphabetical characters **XYX′** that hold the high point of section **A–a′** where John stated the reason God sent John to bear witness— "that all might believe through him" (7^b).

TABLE 5: FOURTH LAYER OF STRUCTURE IN SECTION A: A–a′–cc

			Section A–a′–cc (1:6–8)	
A	**a**		$^{1:1a}$In the beginning was the Word, and the Word was with God,	
	b		$^{1:1b}$and the Word was God.	
	a′	**aa**	^{2}He was in the beginning with God; ^{3}all things were made through him, and without him was not anything made that was made.	
		bb	^{4}In him was life, and the life was the light of everyone. ^{5}The light shines in the darkness, and the darkness has not overcome it.	
		cc	**X**	^{6}There was a man sent from God, whose name was John. ^{7a}He came for testimony, to **bear witness to the light,**
			Y	^{7b}that all might believe through him.
			X′	^{8}He was not the light, but came to **bear witness to the light.**
		bb′	^{9}The true light that enlightens everyone was coming into the world.	
		aa′	^{10}He was in the world, and the world was made through him, yet the world knew him not.	

CLIMAX OF SECTION A

We have progressed spirally to the point in the structure where John shifted topics to say John the Baptist would bear witness to the light, but the author didn't say what the testimony would enable people to believe. This is answered in **table 6** below that displays all passages in section **A**. In **A–b**, the point-of-prominence, the climax, of section **A**, John stated, "the Word was God." This is the theme of the entire Gospel.

> *...but these are written that **you may believe** that Jesus is the Christ, the Son of God, and that believing you may have life in his name* (Jn 20:30).

TABLE 6: SUMMARY OF THE STRUCTURAL ELEMENTS OF SECTION A

				Section A Structured (1:1–10)
A		**a**		[1:1a]In the beginning was the Word, and the Word was with God,
		b		[1:1b]and the Word was God.
	a′	**aa**		[2]He was in the beginning with God; [3]all things were made through him, and without him was not anything made that was made.
		bb		[4]In him was life, and the life was the light of everyone. [5]The light shines in the darkness, and the darkness has not overcome it.
		cc	**X**	[6]There was a man sent from God, whose name was John. [7a]He came for testimony, to bear witness to the light,
			Y	[7b]that all might believe through him.
			X′	[8]He was not the light, but came to bear witness to the light.
		bb′		[9]The true light that enlightens everyone was coming into the world.
		aa′		[10]He was in the world, and the world was made through him, yet the world knew him not.

Why is this crucial passage located near the beginning of section **A**? We normally think of the climax coming at the end of a narrative, and it does when you consider the passages the same way a first-century audience did. The arrows in **table 6** above indicate the path they took. Their mental progression was like a spiral that curved

inward from the outer extremities, going from **A– a** to **A– a′** and their substructures landing between **A– a** and **A– a′** where the POP **A– b** is located.[11]

---

[11] John Breck, *The Shape of Biblical language: Chiasmus in the Scriptures and Beyond*, 57

Part 4
The Value of Structural Analysis

THE EFFORT/REWARD BALANCE

With this introduction to John's structuring style, we ask, is it worth the effort to labor through this detail? You might think the answer is, *No; where's the benefit?* At this point, we agree—the effort outweighs the reward, and if this does not change, literary structural analysis will once again hit a dead end. We liken this situation to that of a musical composer who labors extensively to create a great symphony, but what is its value if no one hears it?

Just as composers notate their music for musicians to play it, scholars, too, must identify and display the aural cues visually. Microsoft Word tables are excellent for scholarly analysis. They provide a way to see John's aural markers that can lead to a completely new context to glean meaning. However, tables are *not* an effective display format for readers. People don't go to the concert hall to have sheet music handed out to them; they go to hear the music played.

THE SITUATION TODAY

Modern readers expect to read Scripture that looks like scripture, not tables. Even if John's writings were read to them, they would not be able to pick up on aural cues as first-century people did. Scholar Breck acknowledged the strong listening skills of first-century listeners and their familiarity with Semitic literary styles that enabled them to hear aural cues that modern listeners miss.

> *The real meaning of the passages cannot be discerned unless we* **read it "spirally,"** *from the extremities toward the center...to the minds of the ancients, this inversion would have posed no problem,*

*for they were trained...to read from the center outward and from
the extremities towards the center...*[12]

Richard Moulton, the father of the literary analysis of the Bible, recognized
the need for visual display of literary structures to ascertain meaning.

*The essential thing is that the **verse structure should be
represented to the eye**...where structural arrangement is wanting,
no amount of explanation is likely to be of much avail.*[13]

Today's readers do see and read John's words as they were read to first-
century listeners, so what are these scholars talking about?

THE PROBLEM

The problem is that modern readers expect the verses to make sense as they
are currently presented in Scripture, but first-century listeners "connected
the dots" differently to derive John's meaning. They used aural cues that
arrived in a spiral progression. Without having a visual depiction of what
the first-century people did mentally, modern readers can't connect the
context clues the same way that first-century listeners did.

Modern readers are simply not "on the same page" and cannot get
there because they do not realize that there is another sequence to use to
take John's message in, and therein lies the source of confusion and
misunderstanding that impairs a modern reader's ability to understand
what John wrote. The reason Moulton said the verse structure must be
made visible is that first-century listeners connected repetitive passages in
their minds where it was never visible! They did it because they were
steeped in the Semitic way of listening.

WHAT IS AT STAKE?

If people can be so moved by hearing a great musical composition that they
stand to offer their applause, imagine the impact of lives changed by
firsthand reading and understanding of John the beloved disciple's

---

[12] John Breck, *The Shape of Biblical language: Chiasmus in the Scriptures and Beyond,* 29–35
[13] Richard G. Moulton, *The Literary Study of the Bible* (London: Heath & Co., 1898) 45

writings! This is only available when twenty-first century readers can read and comprehend John's writings as first-century listeners heard and understood them.

The conundrum is that literary structures portrayed in tables are the equivalent of giving sheet music to a symphony audience. The pivotal question is, how can scholars communicate the spiral verse progression that is in tables to modern readers who can neither read the tables nor want to because they expect to receive John's message as they always have, by reading Scripture that looks like scripture.

THE SOLUTION

If you consider that first-century listeners made a "spiral language" out of the aural cues that they heard, then twenty-first century readers need a translation of that spiral language into a "linear language" that they are familiar with yet incorporates what first-century people heard and understood. This is not different from translating the Bible from another language into English that would take place before writing the scriptural text.

To accomplish this, we created a table to convert the passages in the structures (the layers of cells) from **table 6** into a new sequence where the parallel passages are combined as the early listeners would have done when they heard them. The translation process shown in **table 7,** below, functions like a television relay station. It translates what was programmed in the frequency that first-century listeners used (spiral text) to rebroadcast as linear text for twenty-first-century readers.[14]

---

[14] John Breck, *The Shape of Biblical language: Chiasmus in the Scriptures and Beyond,* 38–39

TABLE 7: TRANSLATION OF SECTION A'S SPIRAL TEXT (RSV) TO LINEAR TEXT (RSAV)

			Section A (1:1–10) Translated	
A	**a**			[1a]In the beginning was the Word, and the Word was with God.
	a'	**aa**		[2]He was in the beginning with God; [3]all things were made through him, and without him was not anything made that was made.
		aa'		[10]He was in the world, and the world was made through him, yet the world knew him not.
		bb		[4]In him was life, and the life was the light of everyone. [5]The light shines in the darkness, and the darkness has not overcome it.
		bb'		[9]The true light that enlightens everyone was coming into the world.
		cc	**X**	[6]There was a man sent from God, whose name was John. [7a]He came for testimony, to bear witness to the light.
			X'	[8]He was not the light, but came to bear witness to the light
			Y	[7b]that all might believe through him.
	b			[1:1b]the word was God

EXTRACTION AND DISPLAY

We extract the passages from the translator table in the exact order they appear there and place them in a format that modern readers are familiar with, which is displayed in **chart 1** below. **The translator table and this chart are the breakthrough innovations** that make the results of a structural analysis of John's writings practical and accessible to all. With it, modern readers have access to the rebroadcast of John's aural structures to enable them to understand his message as naturally as his aural audiences did!

The headlines are an important part of this translation because they display the logic of the message that John's structured writing conveys. They clarify the purpose of his poetic prose.

CHART 1: SECTION A'S (1:1–10) SPIRAL RSV TEXT TRANSLATED TO LINEAR RSAV TEXT

The Word of God
The Word Was in the World That Knew Him Not

[1:1a]In the beginning was the Word and the Word was with God. [2]He was in the beginning with God; [3]all things were made through him, and without him was not anything made that was made. [10]He was in the world, and the world was made through him, yet the world knew him not.

The Word Was Coming into the World

[4]In him was life, and the life was the light of everyone. [5]The light shines in the darkness, and the darkness has not overcome it. [9]The true light that enlightens everyone was coming into the world.

God Sent John to Bear Witness That the Word Was God

[6]There was a man sent from God, whose name was John. [7a]He came for testimony, to bear witness to the light. [8]He was not the light, but came to bear witness to the light, [7b]that all might believe through him: [1:1b]the Word was God.

RSAV TEXT

We call the text in **chart 1** RSAV text (Revised Standard Aural Version) because it uses the RSV second edition for translation from Greek to English as its base. RSV provides the following advantages:

- it is closer to the original Greek writings than many other translations, and
- it incorporates more recently discovered ancient Greek manuscripts of the New Testament.[15]

---

[15] *The New Oxford Annotated Bible with the Apocrypha*, Revised Standard Version, containing the second edition of the New Testament, edited by Herbert G. May & Bruce Metzger (New York: Oxford University Press, 1977)

RSAV is spiral text translated to linear text that delivers the understanding of John's writings that his first-century audience had.

THIS IS A BREAKTHROUGH!

When you consider that a breakthrough is the removal of an impediment or barrier to progress, the RSAV text displayed as it is above is a huge breakthrough. It delivers John's words so coherently that they reveal his meaning without requiring readers to do any additional structural analysis. The reading of this text provides a new level of continuity that offers insights that solve mysteries scholars have pondered for centuries.

RSAV text is a practical and replicable delivery vehicle that brings clarity and reading ease that Johannine scholars have been looking for all along! So why didn't scholars pick up on it when so many advocated for the visual display of literary structures? One reason is that it goes against prevailing norms, a classic roadblock to the pursuit of new ideas, as Galileo's support of a sun-centered solar system exemplified.[16]

However, our quest for a practical and value-added way to make John's writings clear led us to pick up where other scholars left off, to do the "unthinkable"—to display spiral text in a linear format. Our readers strongly confirm the benefits we claim. Their positive responses foretell the potential to dramatically sway the balance of the effort/reward equation of literary structural analysis over to the reward side.

---

[16] http://www.biography.com/people/galileo-9305220#reaction-by-the-church

Part 5
Identification of Substructures in the Rest of the "Prologue"

IDENTIFICATION OF SUBSTRUCTURES IN SECTION A′

We start our investigation into section **A′** by looking for shifts in topic. The author's mention of John who bore witness in v. 15 is the type of break in continuity that indicates vv. 14–18 formulate a three-part structure with **A′–b** sandwiched between the parallel elements **A′–a** and **A′–a′** as the point-of-prominence shown in **table 8** below. The boundaries of the parallel elements **A′–a** and **A′–a′** are marked by the following words.

- "**full**" and "**fullness**" in vv. 14 (πλήρης) and 16 (πληρώματος)
- "**grace and truth**" in vv. 14 and 16 (χάριτος καὶ ἀληθείας)
- "**the only Son**" in vv. 14 (μονογενοῦς) and 18 (μονογενῆ)

TABLE 8: SECOND LAYER OF STRUCTURE IN SECTION A′

		Section A′ (1:14–18)
A′	**a**	[14]And the Word became flesh and dwelt among us, **full** of **grace and truth**; we have beheld his glory, glory as of **the only Son** from the Father.
	b	[15]John bore witness to him, and cried, "This was he of whom I said, 'He who comes after me ranks before me, for he was before me.'"
	a′	[16]And from his **fullness** we have all received, grace upon grace. [17a]For the law was given through Moses; [17b]**grace and truth** came through Jesus Christ. [18a]No one has ever seen God. [18b]**The only Son**, who is in the bosom of the Father, [18c] he has made him known.

Table 9 below displays the third layer of substructures of **A′** contained in **A′–a** and **A′–a′** indicated by the double letters in the third column.

1. The third layer of structure in **A′–a** is defined by a method we have not discussed before. Scholar Dorsey refers to it as topic repetition,[17] which is a repetition of two separate phrases that mean the same thing. In this case, John identifies "**Word became flesh**" and "**the only Son**" as equivalents, and as such, they serve as aural cues that define the boundaries of **A′–a–aa** and **A′–a–aa′**. This technique enables John to make the important point—the only Son of God is the Word.

2. In **A′–a′** the repetition of the word "**grace**" in vv. 16 and 17b establishes the parallel pair of **A′–a′–aa** and **A′–a′–aa′**. The abrupt shift in topic in v. 17a concerning the law given through Moses identifies this passage as the point-of-prominence. It is labeled as **A′–a′–bb**.

TABLE 9: THIRD LAYER OF STRUCTURE IN SECTION A′: A′–A AND A′–A′

			Section A′ Structured (1:14–18)
A′	a	aa	[14a]And the **Word became flesh** and dwelt among us,
		bb	[14b]full of grace and truth;
		aa′	[14c]we have beheld his glory, glory as of **the only Son** from the Father.
	b		[15](John bore witness to him, and cried, "This was he of whom I said, 'He who comes after me ranks before me, for he was before me.'")
	a′	aa	[16]And from his fullness we have all received, **grace** upon grace.
		bb	[17a]For the law was given through Moses;
		aa′	[17b]**grace** and truth came through Jesus Christ. [18a]No one has ever seen God. [18b]The only Son, who is in the bosom

[17] David A. Dorsey, *The Literary Structure of the Old Testament: A commentary on Genesis–Malachi* (Grand Rapids: Baker Books, 1999) 18

Section A´ Structured (1:14–18)			
			of the Father, ¹⁸ᶜhe has made him known.

The fourth layer of structure in section **A´** is located within **A´– a´– aa´** shown in **table 10** below. Once again, John uses topic repetition to mark it. He links "**Jesus Christ**" (v. 17b) to "**the only Son**" (v. 18b).

TABLE 10: FOURTH LAYER OF STRUCTURE IN SECTION A´: A´–A´–AA´

Section A´–a´–aa´ (1:17b–18)				
			X	¹⁷ᵇGrace and truth came through **Jesus Christ.**
A´	**a´**	**aa´**	**Y**	¹⁸ᵃNo one has ever seen God.
			X´	¹⁸ᵇThe **only Son,** who is in the bosom of the Father, ¹⁸ᶜhe has made him known.

IDENTIFICATION OF SUBSTRUCTURES IN SECTION B

The repetitive phrase "**received him**" (vv. 11 and 12) marks the parallel elements **B–a** and **B–a´** shown in **table 11**. The topic break in **B–b** indicates that it is the point-of-prominence, but it is *not* located between two parallel elements as is typical. What we have here is a "specific-to-general" structure where the parallel elements **B–a** and **B–a´** deal with the specifics:

- Those who do *not* receive Jesus
- Those who do receive Jesus

The point-of-prominence that follows as another substructure is the general statement because the opportunity to become a child of God applies to everyone. John uses this point-of-prominence to state the new way to become a child of God.

TABLE 11: SECOND AND THIRD LAYERS OF STRUCTURE IN SECTION B

			Section B Structured (1:11–13)
B	**a**		[11]He came to his own home, and his own people **received him not.**
	a'		[12]But to all who **received Him,** who believed in His name, he gave power to become children of God,
	b	**aa**	[13a]who were born,
		bb	[13b]not of blood, nor of the will of the flesh, nor of the will of man,
		aa'	[13c]of God.

The third-layer structure **B–b** in **table 11** above is not based on word repetition but on thought continuation.[18] It is indicated by the double-letter labels. The first parallel **B–b–aa** introduces the topic of birth. The parallel complement **B–b–aa'** continues John's discussion about birth. The point-of-prominence **B– b–bb** states that becoming a child of God is not by any means in the purview of humans. The parallel pair makes it clear that it is granted by God.

---

[18] Dorsey, *Literary Structure of the Old Testament,* 18

Part 6

Translation of the "Prologue" From RSV to RSAV Text

SUMMARY OF THE AURAL STRUCTURES OF THE "PROLOGUE"

All the passages of the "Prologue" are summarized in their layered structures in **table 12,** below. They are sequenced as first-century listeners heard them spoken and as readers see and read the "Prologue" today. However, first-century listeners understood these passages as spiral text, which means they mentally associated the repetitive passages with each other to enhance their understanding.

Therefore, to bring modern readers onto the same page as first-century listeners, this text needs to be translated into text that takes aural cues into account, which we call RSAV (Revised Standard Aural Version). This takes place in a translator table, **table 13** that follows **table 12,** below.

TABLE 12: SUMMARY OF ALL STRUCTURES OF THE "PROLOGUE" DISPLAYED AS SPIRAL TEXT

				The "Prologue" (RSV)—All Levels of Structure (1:1–18)
A		**a**		[1a]In the beginning was the Word, and the Word was with God,
		b		[1b]and the Word was God.
	a′	**aa**		[2]He was in the beginning with God; [3]all things were made through him, and without him was not anything made that was made.
		bb		[4]In him was life, and the life was the light of everyone. [5]The light shines in the darkness, and the darkness has not overcome it.
		cc	**X**	[6]There was a man sent from God, whose name was John. [7a]He came for testimony, to bear witness to the light,
			Y	[7b]that all might believe through him.
			X′	[8]He was not the light, but came to bear witness to the light.
		bb′		[9]The true light that enlightens everyone was coming into the world.
		aa′		[10]He was in the world, and the world was made through him, yet the world knew him not.
B	**a**			[11]He came to his own home, and his own people received him not.
	a′			[12]But to all who received Him, who believed in His name, he gave power to become children of God,
	b	**aa**		[13a]who were born,
		bb		[13b]not of blood, nor of the will of the flesh, nor of the will of man,
		aa′		[13c]of God.
A′	**a**	**aa**		[14a]And the Word became flesh and dwelt among us,
		bb		[14b]full of grace and truth;
		aa′		[14c]we have beheld his glory, glory as of the only Son from the Father.
	b			[15](John bore witness to him, and cried, "This was he of whom I said, 'He who comes after me ranks before me, for he was

The "Prologue" (RSV)—All Levels of Structure (1:1–18)				
		before me.'")		
		aa	¹⁶And from his fullness we have all received, grace upon grace.	
		bb	¹⁷ᵃFor the law was given through Moses;	
	a′		X	¹⁷ᵇgrace and truth came through Jesus Christ.
		aa′	Y	¹⁸ᵃNo one has ever seen God.
			X′	¹⁸ᵇThe only Son, who is in the bosom of the Father, ¹⁸ᶜhe has made him known.

THE TRANSLATOR TABLE

The translator table converts the passages in the structures (the layers of cells) from **table 12,** above, into the sequence shown in **table 13,** below. It places the parallel passages together as the early listeners did when they heard them. The points-of-prominence are positioned in relation to the parallel pairs in accord with how first-century listeners mentally packaged them.[19] The result is the "Prologue" converted to linear text (RSAV)[20] that is displayed in **chart 2** that follows **table 13.**

---

[19] John Breck, *The Shape of Biblical language: Chiasmus in the Scriptures and Beyond,* 38–39

[20] RSAV text is derived from the highly-regarded RSV translation whereby the RSAV converts the RSV into an aural formulation as first-century listeners heard and understood it.

TABLE 13: THE "PROLOGUE" RSV (SPIRAL TEXT) TRANSLATED TO RSAV (LINEAR TEXT)

				The "Prologue" (RSV)—All Structures (1:1–18)
A	**a**			[1a]In the beginning was the Word, and the Word was with God,
	a′	**aa**		[2]He was in the beginning with God; [3]all things were made through him, and without him was not anything made that was made.
		aa′		[10]He was in the world, and the world was made through him, yet the world knew him not.
		bb		[4]In him was life, and the life was the light of everyone. [5]The light shines in the darkness, and the darkness has not overcome it.
		bb′		[9]The true light that enlightens everyone was coming into the world.
		cc	**X**	[6]There was a man sent from God, whose name was John. [7a]He came for testimony, to bear witness to the light,
			X′	[8]He was not the light, but came to bear witness to the light.
			Y	[7b]that all might believe through him.
	b			[1b]and the Word was God.
A′	**a**	**aa**		[14a]And the Word became flesh and dwelt among us,
		aa′		[14c]we have beheld his glory, glory as of the only Son from the Father.
		bb		[14b]full of grace and truth;
	a′	**aa**		[16]And from his fullness we have all received, grace upon grace.
		aa′	**X**	[17b]grace and truth came through Jesus Christ.
			X′	[18b]The only Son, who is in the bosom of the Father, [18c]he has made him known.
			Y	[18a]No one has ever seen God.
		bb		[17a]For the law was given through Moses;

	b	¹⁵(John bore witness to him, and cried, "This was he of whom I said, 'He who comes after me ranks before me, for he was before me.'")
	a	¹¹He came to his own home, and his own people received him not.
B	**a′**	¹²But to all who received Him, who believed in His name, he gave power to become children of God,
	aa	¹³ªwho were born,
b	**aa′**	¹³ᶜof God.
	bb	¹³ᵇnot of blood, nor of the will of the flesh, nor of the will of man,

EXTRACTION OF THE "PROLOGUE" TO RSAV TEXT

We extract the passages from the translator table in the exact sequence they appear there and place them in a format that modern readers are familiar with that is displayed in **chart 2** below. We call the extracted passages RSAV (Revised Standard Aural Version) because it is spiral text converted to linear sequence that incorporates John's aural cues.

RSAV text enables modern readers to read a rebroadcast of the composer's (John's) spiral text to understand his message as naturally as John's aural audiences did. This translator table and chart are the breakthrough innovations that make the results of a structural analysis of John's writings practical and accessible to all. They are the affirmative answer to the question we posed earlier: "Is literary structural analysis worth the effort?" Yes!

THE HEADLINES

Before you start to read the RSAV text below, please note that its headlines are intended to be more than simple attention-getters. They are an important part of the exegesis by doing the following:

- Organizing and unifying the text to orient the reader
- Revealing the key message of the text
- Providing a quick way to understand the text
- Clarifying the purpose of John's poetic prose

The three major headlines listed in bold below provide an accurate and logical synthesis of God's plan with its overriding theme of salvation.

1. **The Word of God** introduces the world's problem and the solution that was coming, who would be the light, who is the Word, who is God, and who will become flesh and give everyone the opportunity to enlighten.

2. **Two Witnesses of the Word** introduces John the Evangelist who beheld Jesus's glory and John the Baptist who was sent by God for witness. Without their eyewitness accounts, no one would believe Jesus Christ is the Son of God who makes God known.

3. **All Who Believe Have the Power to Become Born of God** proclaims the new opportunity available to all who receive and believe in Jesus's name to become children of God.

CHART 2: "PROLOGUE" (1:1–18) RSV SPIRAL IN RSAV SEQUENCE

The Word of God
The Word Was in the World That Knew Him Not

^{1a}In the beginning was the Word and the Word was with God. ^{2}He was in the beginning with God; ^{3}all things were made through him, and without him was not anything made that was made. ^{10}He was in the world, and the world was made through him, yet the world knew him not.

The Word Was Coming into the World

^{4}In him was life, and the life was the light of everyone. ^{5}The light shines in the darkness, and the darkness has not overcome it. ^{9}The true light that enlightens everyone was coming into the world.

God Sent John to Bear Witness That the Word Was God

^{6}There was a man sent from God, whose name was John. ^{7a}He came for testimony, to bear witness to the light. ^{8}He was not the light, but came to bear witness to the light, [7b]that all might believe through him: [1b]the Word was God, [14a]and the Word became flesh and dwelt among us.

Two Witnesses of the Word
John the Evangelist Testified That Jesus Is the Son of God

[4c]We have beheld his glory, glory as of the only Son from the Father [14b]full of grace and truth. [16]And from his fullness, we have all received, grace upon grace. [17b]Grace and truth came through Jesus Christ, [18b]the only Son, who is in the bosom of the Father, [18c]he has made him known. [18a]No one has ever seen God, [17a] for the law was given through Moses.

John the Baptist Bore Witness That the Son of God Is Jesus

[15]John bore witness to him, and cried, "This was he of whom I said, 'He who comes after me ranks before me, for he was before me.'"

All Who Believe Have the Power to Become Born of God

[11]He came to his own home, and his own people received him not.[12]But to all who received Him, who believed in His name, he gave power to become children of God; [13a]who were born [13c]of God, [13b]not of blood, nor of the will of the flesh, nor of the will of man.

Part 7

Six New Perspectives of the "Prologue"

INTRODUCTION TO THE BENEFITS

The RSAV "Prologue" alleviates confusing points, provides a more logical flow, contributes greater clarity, and clearly imparts the purpose of the Gospel. RSAV text provides these benefits without sacrificing the beauty of the prose. We organize our explanation according to the headlines shown in **chart 2** on the prior pages.

THE WORD OF GOD

This section places the focus on who the Word is, what he came to do, and that he will do it as a human.

1. **The Word Was in the World That Knew Him Not**

    The aural text's inclusion of v. 10 in this opening section brings the dynamic purpose of the Gospel forth by stating the predicament— the world did not know its Maker and had not since Adam and Eve committed the sin that led to their and their progeny's banishment (Gen 22–24). With rare exceptions, no one could know God during the banishment period. John did not imply that the world was amiss or ungrateful for not knowing its creator[21] nor was he condemning the world. Instead, his statement of this fact set up what was to follow.

2. **The Word Was Coming into the World**

    This section alleviates confusion about how the Creator Word could already be in the world and at the same time be coming into the world. The Word who was coming was going to be different

---

[21] Gail R. O'Day, "The Gospel of John: Introduction, Commentary, and Reflections," *NIB* (Nashville: Abingdon Press, 1995) 9:521

from the Word who was the maker of all things. He would be a new manifestation of the Word—the life and light who would solve the problem of not knowing God.

3. **God Sent John to Bear Witness That the Word Was God**

This section answers the question of how people would be able to recognize the light who was going to look like and live with other humans as the Word. John the Baptist was going to identify and bear witness to the Word who became a man as being God so people would know who their savior was and would believe. The problem in other translations is that vv. 6–8 interrupt the flow such that some scholars question their very inclusion in the "Prologue".[22] However, the flow of the RSAV text provides the continuity that reveals the necessity of John the Baptist's testimony.

TWO WITNESSES

This section places the focus on two powerful witnesses of Jesus being the Son of God. John the Evangelist provides the first witness that Jesus is the Son of God; John the Baptist follows by declaring that Jesus ranks before him.

4. **John the Evangelist Testified That Jesus Is the Son of God**

In the early centuries, after Jesus's death and resurrection, people hotly debated whether Jesus was only human, only Divine, or both. John who was Jesus's beloved disciple knew Jesus as human, and here he compellingly substantiates that Jesus was both human and Divine by his eyewitness testimony that he and the other disciples beheld Jesus in his glory. They saw, heard, and physically received his supreme gift of grace. By this, they finally knew Jesus was the truth—the only Son of God.

> *On the evening of that day... where the disciples were...Jesus came and stood among them and said to*

---

[22] Raymond E. Brown, *The Gospel According to John, I–XII* (AB 29; New York: Doubleday, 1966) 27–28

them, "Peace be with you." When he had said this, he showed them his hands and his side...he breathed on them, and said to them, "Receive the Holy Spirit" (Jn 20:19–20, 22b RSV).

John's mention of the law being given through Moses meant that not even the chosen people could see or know God. They couldn't have seen God because the law was given to them through Moses, not from God directly. However, John and the disciples saw God face-to-face! This was their final preparation to become Jesus's appointed messengers to convey the opportunity for everyone to receive eternal life and to eventually see God face-to-face.

*And this is eternal life, that they **know** thee the only true God, and Jesus Christ whom thou has sent* (Jn 17:27 RSAV).

5. **John the Baptist Bore Witness That the Son of God Is Jesus**
   With John the Baptist's testimony coming after John the Evangelist's proclamation that Jesus is the only Son of the Father, readers would understand why John the Baptist would proclaim that Jesus ranks before him. The RSAV text presents the two testimonies in a more logical progression than other translations where the testimonies are intermixed.

ALL WHO BELIEVE HAVE THE POWER TO BECOME BORN OF GOD

6. Verses 11–13 in the RSAV are the same as other translations; however, the RSAV provides a benefit by its placement of these passages because they carry the reader toward this climatic high point that all are included in God's plan for salvation. To know God eternally as a birthright has been replaced by the choice that Jesus made possible for everyone. They have the choice to receive Jesus and believe in his name.

Part 8
Conclusion

VISIBLE STRUCTURES REVEAL THE PATH THROUGH THE MAZE

We conclude by giving Richard Moulton, the father of literary analysis, the final word. A nineteenth-century scholar from the University of Chicago who brought the existence of aural structures in the Bible to the forefront, Moulton states, "The essential thing is that the verse structure should be represented to the eye...where structural arrangement is wanting, no amount of explanation is likely to be of much avail."[23]

When one considers the number of pages that continue to be written with new interpretive angles on the "Prologue," scholars essentially have proved Mouton right. Surely John would never have intended to be so obtuse. For example, would he have inserted passages that refer to John the Baptist in a confusing sequence. Who does John say saw Jesus's glory? What are people to believe? We have demonstrated how just one shift in perception—to that of linearly sequenced text that incorporates aural structures—can bring textual coherence that reveals long-sought answers to interpretive questions. Moulton's invitation to religious scholars was to experience what a mathematician who finally sees an orderly pattern in what appears to be a set of random numbers experiences.

The newfound clarity that RSAV text brings to the "Prologue" demonstrates why Moulton would make such a statement; however, even innovations that offer obvious advantages face great difficulty in becoming adopted. Everett Rogers cites Machiavelli: "There is nothing more difficult to plan, more doubtful of success, more dangerous to manage than the

---

[23] R. G. Moulton, *The Literary Study of the Bible* (Lexington, Mass.: Heath, 1898) 45

creation of a new order of things."[24] Without a doubt, adoption of RSAV text for exegesis has encountered such resistance.

THE FINAL QUESTION

Will the three methods we advocate—

- word and topic repetition and breaks in continuity for decoding,
- layering in Microsoft Word tables for creation and integration of structures, and
- a nontechnical display format with RSAV text—

be enough to rekindle scholarly interest?

Innovation presents scholars with a new means to solve problems, to make discoveries, and to bring further hope to an ever-ready audience. We attest to the value of the aural structures that inform John's Gospel and Epistles in *Jesus's Beloved Disciple Calling Seize Life Now*.[25] We conclude that since every New Testament author wrote for transmission to an aural audience, a barely tapped field of structural analysis for exegesis awaits the fresh revelations scholars could bring to light.

---

[24] Rodgers, *Diffusion of Innovations*, 1; Niccolò Machiavelli, *The Prince* (trans. N. H. Thomson; New York: Dover, 1992) 13

[25] Lou Mertes and Nicole Mertes, *Jesus's Beloved Disciple Calling Seize Life Now!* (Bellevue, WA: The Impact Organization, Inc., 2016)

About the Authors

Lou and Nicole Mertes

Lou and Nicole have served on the Seattle Pacific Seminary Advisory Council and are directors of the Bible Reading Breakthrough™ Project, a ministry dedicated to bringing enthusiasm back to Bible study. Their work enables today's readers:

- to comprehend God's word as the original audiences would have heard and understood it,
- to provide more clarity and accuracy of interpretation, and
- to more fully engage in Bible study.

When they are not writing, they compete in tall-building-stair-climbing fund-raising events.

About Lou

Lou brings the same innovative spirit to the detection and display of John's literary structures that he was recognized for throughout his career as a chief information executive. He was recognized in *Time* magazine's 1983 "Computer of the Year" issue for spearheading the largest implementation of e-mail and office automation to that date. He authored a *Harvard Business Review* article on that topic that was one of the most requested reprints. He was invited to speak worldwide and to contribute to the book *Communications in the Twenty-first Century*.

While completing his degree in theology in 2006, Lou was introduced to literary analysis of the Bible. His ensuing ten years of experimentation led to the breakthrough that enables today's readers to comprehend John's writings with more clarity.

About Nicole

Nicole saw the potential for managers to become catalysts for change that led to her founding a company to provide instructional and software products for ongoing improvement initiatives. During the company's twenty-eight years, thousands of clients received raises, bonuses, and promotions by putting the techniques she developed into practice. She taught at the University of Wisconsin's summer program for seven years. Her company's vanguard software was endorsed by the American Bankers Association and featured on the cover of *Quality Digest*.

Nicole is the designer of eight instructional products, one receiving the highest award for instructional excellence from the International Society for Performance and Instruction. Today, she relishes collaborating with Lou by writing about his research to facilitate people's realization of the inspiring power of the Bible to live the great command to love one another.

www.ingramcontent.com/pod-product-compliance
Lightning Source LLC
Chambersburg PA
CBHW060634030426
42337CB00018B/3365